INITIAL GOAL	Write the goal you have in mind

S SPECIFIC	What do you want to accomplish? Who needs to be included? When do you want to do this? Why is this a goal?

M MEASURABLE	How can you measure progress and know if you've successfully met your goal?

A ACHIEVABLE	Do you have the skills required to achieve the goal? If not, can you obtain them? What is the motivation for this goal? Is the amount of effort required on par with what the goal will achieve?

R RELEVANT	Why am I setting this goal now? Is it aligned with overall objectives?

T TIME-BOUND	What's the deadline and is it realistic?

SMART GOAL	Review what you have written, and craft a new goal statement based on what the answers to the questions above have revealed

INITIAL GOAL	Write the goal you have in mind

S **SPECIFIC**	What do you want to accomplish? Who needs to be included? When do you want to do this? Why is this a goal?

M **MEASURABLE**	How can you measure progress and know if you've successfully met your goal?

A **ACHIEVABLE**	Do you have the skills required to achieve the goal? If not, can you obtain them? What is the motivation for this goal? Is the amount of effort required on par with what the goal will achieve?

R **RELEVANT**	Why am I setting this goal now? Is it aligned with overall objectives?

T **TIME-BOUND**	What's the deadline and is it realistic?

SMART GOAL	Review what you have written, and craft a new goal statement based on what the answers to the questions above have revealed

INITIAL GOAL	Write the goal you have in mind

S **SPECIFIC**	What do you want to accomplish? Who needs to be included? When do you want to do this? Why is this a goal?

M **MEASURABLE**	How can you measure progress and know if you've successfully met your goal?

A **ACHIEVABLE**	Do you have the skills required to achieve the goal? If not, can you obtain them? What is the motivation for this goal? Is the amount of effort required on par with what the goal will achieve?

R **RELEVANT**	Why am I setting this goal now? Is it aligned with overall objectives?

T **TIME-BOUND**	What's the deadline and is it realistic?

SMART GOAL	Review what you have written, and craft a new goal statement based on what the answers to the questions above have revealed

INITIAL GOAL	Write the goal you have in mind
S	What do you want to accomplish? Who needs to be included? When do you want to do this? Why is this a goal?
SPECIFIC	
M	How can you measure progress and know if you've successfully met your goal?
MEASURABLE	
A	Do you have the skills required to achieve the goal? If not, can you obtain them? What is the motivation for this goal? Is the amount of effort required on par with what the goal will achieve?
ACHIEVABLE	
R	Why am I setting this goal now? Is it aligned with overall objectives?
RELEVANT	
T	What's the deadline and is it realistic?
TIME-BOUND	
SMART GOAL	Review what you have written, and craft a new goal statement based on what the answers to the questions above have revealed

INITIAL GOAL

Write the goal you have in mind

S
SPECIFIC

What do you want to accomplish? Who needs to be included? When do you want to do this? Why is this a goal?

M
MEASURABLE

How can you measure progress and know if you've successfully met your goal?

A
ACHIEVABLE

Do you have the skills required to achieve the goal? If not, can you obtain them? What is the motivation for this goal? Is the amount of effort required on par with what the goal will achieve?

R
RELEVANT

Why am I setting this goal now? Is it aligned with overall objectives?

T
TIME-BOUND

What's the deadline and is it realistic?

SMART GOAL

Review what you have written, and craft a new goal statement based on what the answers to the questions above have revealed

INITIAL GOAL	Write the goal you have in mind
S **SPECIFIC**	What do you want to accomplish? Who needs to be included? When do you want to do this? Why is this a goal?
M **MEASURABLE**	How can you measure progress and know if you've successfully met your goal?
A **ACHIEVABLE**	Do you have the skills required to achieve the goal? If not, can you obtain them? What is the motivation for this goal? Is the amount of effort required on par with what the goal will achieve?
R **RELEVANT**	Why am I setting this goal now? Is it aligned with overall objectives?
T **TIME-BOUND**	What's the deadline and is it realistic?
SMART GOAL	Review what you have written, and craft a new goal statement based on what the answers to the questions above have revealed

INITIAL GOAL	Write the goal you have in mind

S **SPECIFIC**	What do you want to accomplish? Who needs to be included? When do you want to do this? Why is this a goal?

M **MEASURABLE**	How can you measure progress and know if you've successfully met your goal?

A **ACHIEVABLE**	Do you have the skills required to achieve the goal? If not, can you obtain them? What is the motivation for this goal? Is the amount of effort required on par with what the goal will achieve?

R **RELEVANT**	Why am I setting this goal now? Is it aligned with overall objectives?

T **TIME-BOUND**	What's the deadline and is it realistic?

SMART GOAL	Review what you have written, and craft a new goal statement based on what the answers to the questions above have revealed

INITIAL GOAL	Write the goal you have in mind
S **SPECIFIC**	What do you want to accomplish? Who needs to be included? When do you want to do this? Why is this a goal?
M **MEASURABLE**	How can you measure progress and know if you've successfully met your goal?
A **ACHIEVABLE**	Do you have the skills required to achieve the goal? If not, can you obtain them? What is the motivation for this goal? Is the amount of effort required on par with what the goal will achieve?
R **RELEVANT**	Why am I setting this goal now? Is it aligned with overall objectives?
T **TIME-BOUND**	What's the deadline and is it realistic?
SMART GOAL	Review what you have written, and craft a new goal statement based on what the answers to the questions above have revealed

INITIAL GOAL	Write the goal you have in mind

S	What do you want to accomplish? Who needs to be included? When do you want to do this? Why is this a goal?
SPECIFIC	

M	How can you measure progress and know if you've successfully met your goal?
MEASURABLE	

A	Do you have the skills required to achieve the goal? If not, can you obtain them? What is the motivation for this goal? Is the amount of effort required on par with what the goal will achieve?
ACHIEVABLE	

R	Why am I setting this goal now? Is it aligned with overall objectives?
RELEVANT	

T	What's the deadline and is it realistic?
TIME-BOUND	

SMART GOAL	Review what you have written, and craft a new goal statement based on what the answers to the questions above have revealed

INITIAL GOAL	Write the goal you have in mind

S	What do you want to accomplish? Who needs to be included? When do you want to do this? Why is this a goal?
SPECIFIC	

M	How can you measure progress and know if you've successfully met your goal?
MEASURABLE	

A	Do you have the skills required to achieve the goal? If not, can you obtain them? What is the motivation for this goal? Is the amount of effort required on par with what the goal will achieve?
ACHIEVABLE	

R	Why am I setting this goal now? Is it aligned with overall objectives?
RELEVANT	

T	What's the deadline and is it realistic?
TIME-BOUND	

SMART GOAL	Review what you have written, and craft a new goal statement based on what the answers to the questions above have revealed

INITIAL GOAL	Write the goal you have in mind
S **SPECIFIC**	What do you want to accomplish? Who needs to be included? When do you want to do this? Why is this a goal?
M **MEASURABLE**	How can you measure progress and know if you've successfully met your goal?
A **ACHIEVABLE**	Do you have the skills required to achieve the goal? If not, can you obtain them? What is the motivation for this goal? Is the amount of effort required on par with what the goal will achieve?
R **RELEVANT**	Why am I setting this goal now? Is it aligned with overall objectives?
T **TIME-BOUND**	What's the deadline and is it realistic?
SMART GOAL	Review what you have written, and craft a new goal statement based on what the answers to the questions above have revealed

INITIAL GOAL	Write the goal you have in mind

S	What do you want to accomplish? Who needs to be included? When do you want to do this? Why is this a goal?
SPECIFIC	

M	How can you measure progress and know if you've successfully met your goal?
MEASURABLE	

A	Do you have the skills required to achieve the goal? If not, can you obtain them? What is the motivation for this goal? Is the amount of effort required on par with what the goal will achieve?
ACHIEVABLE	

R	Why am I setting this goal now? Is it aligned with overall objectives?
RELEVANT	

T	What's the deadline and is it realistic?
TIME-BOUND	

SMART GOAL	Review what you have written, and craft a new goal statement based on what the answers to the questions above have revealed

INITIAL GOAL	Write the goal you have in mind

| S

SPECIFIC	What do you want to accomplish? Who needs to be included? When do you want to do this? Why is this a goal?

| M

MEASURABLE	How can you measure progress and know if you've successfully met your goal?

| A

ACHIEVABLE	Do you have the skills required to achieve the goal? If not, can you obtain them? What is the motivation for this goal? Is the amount of effort required on par with what the goal will achieve?

| R

RELEVANT	Why am I setting this goal now? Is it aligned with overall objectives?

| T

TIME-BOUND	What's the deadline and is it realistic?

SMART GOAL	Review what you have written, and craft a new goal statement based on what the answers to the questions above have revealed

INITIAL GOAL	Write the goal you have in mind
S **SPECIFIC**	What do you want to accomplish? Who needs to be included? When do you want to do this? Why is this a goal?
M **MEASURABLE**	How can you measure progress and know if you've successfully met your goal?
A **ACHIEVABLE**	Do you have the skills required to achieve the goal? If not, can you obtain them? What is the motivation for this goal? Is the amount of effort required on par with what the goal will achieve?
R **RELEVANT**	Why am I setting this goal now? Is it aligned with overall objectives?
T **TIME-BOUND**	What's the deadline and is it realistic?
SMART GOAL	Review what you have written, and craft a new goal statement based on what the answers to the questions above have revealed

| **INITIAL GOAL** | Write the goal you have in mind |
| | |

| **S**
SPECIFIC | What do you want to accomplish? Who needs to be included? When do you want to do this? Why is this a goal? |
| | |

| **M**
MEASURABLE | How can you measure progress and know if you've successfully met your goal? |
| | |

| **A**
ACHIEVABLE | Do you have the skills required to achieve the goal? If not, can you obtain them? What is the motivation for this goal? Is the amount of effort required on par with what the goal will achieve? |
| | |

| **R**
RELEVANT | Why am I setting this goal now? Is it aligned with overall objectives? |
| | |

| **T**
TIME-BOUND | What's the deadline and is it realistic? |
| | |

| **SMART GOAL** | Review what you have written, and craft a new goal statement based on what the answers to the questions above have revealed |
| | |

INITIAL GOAL	Write the goal you have in mind

S	What do you want to accomplish? Who needs to be included? When do you want to do this? Why is this a goal?
SPECIFIC	

M	How can you measure progress and know if you've successfully met your goal?
MEASURABLE	

A	Do you have the skills required to achieve the goal? If not, can you obtain them? What is the motivation for this goal? Is the amount of effort required on par with what the goal will achieve?
ACHIEVABLE	

R	Why am I setting this goal now? Is it aligned with overall objectives?
RELEVANT	

T	What's the deadline and is it realistic?
TIME-BOUND	

SMART GOAL	Review what you have written, and craft a new goal statement based on what the answers to the questions above have revealed

INITIAL GOAL	Write the goal you have in mind
S **SPECIFIC**	What do you want to accomplish? Who needs to be included? When do you want to do this? Why is this a goal?
M **MEASURABLE**	How can you measure progress and know if you've successfully met your goal?
A **ACHIEVABLE**	Do you have the skills required to achieve the goal? If not, can you obtain them? What is the motivation for this goal? Is the amount of effort required on par with what the goal will achieve?
R **RELEVANT**	Why am I setting this goal now? Is it aligned with overall objectives?
T **TIME-BOUND**	What's the deadline and is it realistic?
SMART GOAL	Review what you have written, and craft a new goal statement based on what the answers to the questions above have revealed

INITIAL GOAL	Write the goal you have in mind
S **SPECIFIC**	What do you want to accomplish? Who needs to be included? When do you want to do this? Why is this a goal?
M **MEASURABLE**	How can you measure progress and know if you've successfully met your goal?
A **ACHIEVABLE**	Do you have the skills required to achieve the goal? If not, can you obtain them? What is the motivation for this goal? Is the amount of effort required on par with what the goal will achieve?
R **RELEVANT**	Why am I setting this goal now? Is it aligned with overall objectives?
T **TIME-BOUND**	What's the deadline and is it realistic?
SMART GOAL	Review what you have written, and craft a new goal statement based on what the answers to the questions above have revealed

INITIAL GOAL	Write the goal you have in mind

S **SPECIFIC**	What do you want to accomplish? Who needs to be included? When do you want to do this? Why is this a goal?

M **MEASURABLE**	How can you measure progress and know if you've successfully met your goal?

A **ACHIEVABLE**	Do you have the skills required to achieve the goal? If not, can you obtain them? What is the motivation for this goal? Is the amount of effort required on par with what the goal will achieve?

R **RELEVANT**	Why am I setting this goal now? Is it aligned with overall objectives?

T **TIME-BOUND**	What's the deadline and is it realistic?

SMART GOAL	Review what you have written, and craft a new goal statement based on what the answers to the questions above have revealed

INITIAL GOAL	Write the goal you have in mind

S	What do you want to accomplish? Who needs to be included? When do you want to do this? Why is this a goal?
SPECIFIC	

M	How can you measure progress and know if you've successfully met your goal?
MEASURABLE	

A	Do you have the skills required to achieve the goal? If not, can you obtain them? What is the motivation for this goal? Is the amount of effort required on par with what the goal will achieve?
ACHIEVABLE	

R	Why am I setting this goal now? Is it aligned with overall objectives?
RELEVANT	

T	What's the deadline and is it realistic?
TIME-BOUND	

SMART GOAL	Review what you have written, and craft a new goal statement based on what the answers to the questions above have revealed

INITIAL GOAL	Write the goal you have in mind

S **SPECIFIC**	What do you want to accomplish? Who needs to be included? When do you want to do this? Why is this a goal?

M **MEASURABLE**	How can you measure progress and know if you've successfully met your goal?

A **ACHIEVABLE**	Do you have the skills required to achieve the goal? If not, can you obtain them? What is the motivation for this goal? Is the amount of effort required on par with what the goal will achieve?

R **RELEVANT**	Why am I setting this goal now? Is it aligned with overall objectives?

T **TIME-BOUND**	What's the deadline and is it realistic?

SMART GOAL	Review what you have written, and craft a new goal statement based on what the answers to the questions above have revealed

INITIAL GOAL	Write the goal you have in mind

S SPECIFIC	What do you want to accomplish? Who needs to be included? When do you want to do this? Why is this a goal?

M MEASURABLE	How can you measure progress and know if you've successfully met your goal?

A ACHIEVABLE	Do you have the skills required to achieve the goal? If not, can you obtain them? What is the motivation for this goal? Is the amount of effort required on par with what the goal will achieve?

R RELEVANT	Why am I setting this goal now? Is it aligned with overall objectives?

T TIME-BOUND	What's the deadline and is it realistic?

SMART GOAL	Review what you have written, and craft a new goal statement based on what the answers to the questions above have revealed

INITIAL GOAL	Write the goal you have in mind

S SPECIFIC	What do you want to accomplish? Who needs to be included? When do you want to do this? Why is this a goal?

M MEASURABLE	How can you measure progress and know if you've successfully met your goal?

A ACHIEVABLE	Do you have the skills required to achieve the goal? If not, can you obtain them? What is the motivation for this goal? Is the amount of effort required on par with what the goal will achieve?

R RELEVANT	Why am I setting this goal now? Is it aligned with overall objectives?

T TIME-BOUND	What's the deadline and is it realistic?

SMART GOAL	Review what you have written, and craft a new goal statement based on what the answers to the questions above have revealed

INITIAL GOAL	Write the goal you have in mind
S **SPECIFIC**	What do you want to accomplish? Who needs to be included? When do you want to do this? Why is this a goal?
M **MEASURABLE**	How can you measure progress and know if you've successfully met your goal?
A **ACHIEVABLE**	Do you have the skills required to achieve the goal? If not, can you obtain them? What is the motivation for this goal? Is the amount of effort required on par with what the goal will achieve?.
R **RELEVANT**	Why am I setting this goal now? Is it aligned with overall objectives?
T **TIME-BOUND**	What's the deadline and is it realistic?
SMART GOAL	Review what you have written, and craft a new goal statement based on what the answers to the questions above have revealed

INITIAL GOAL	Write the goal you have in mind

S SPECIFIC	What do you want to accomplish? Who needs to be included? When do you want to do this? Why is this a goal?

M MEASURABLE	How can you measure progress and know if you've successfully met your goal?

A ACHIEVABLE	Do you have the skills required to achieve the goal? If not, can you obtain them? What is the motivation for this goal? Is the amount of effort required on par with what the goal will achieve?

R RELEVANT	Why am I setting this goal now? Is it aligned with overall objectives?

T TIME-BOUND	What's the deadline and is it realistic?

SMART GOAL	Review what you have written, and craft a new goal statement based on what the answers to the questions above have revealed

INITIAL GOAL	Write the goal you have in mind
S **SPECIFIC**	What do you want to accomplish? Who needs to be included? When do you want to do this? Why is this a goal?
M **MEASURABLE**	How can you measure progress and know if you've successfully met your goal?
A **ACHIEVABLE**	Do you have the skills required to achieve the goal? If not, can you obtain them? What is the motivation for this goal? Is the amount of effort required on par with what the goal will achieve?
R **RELEVANT**	Why am I setting this goal now? Is it aligned with overall objectives?
T **TIME-BOUND**	What's the deadline and is it realistic?
SMART GOAL	Review what you have written, and craft a new goal statement based on what the answers to the questions above have revealed

INITIAL GOAL	Write the goal you have in mind

S **SPECIFIC**	What do you want to accomplish? Who needs to be included? When do you want to do this? Why is this a goal?

M **MEASURABLE**	How can you measure progress and know if you've successfully met your goal?

A **ACHIEVABLE**	Do you have the skills required to achieve the goal? If not, can you obtain them? What is the motivation for this goal? Is the amount of effort required on par with what the goal will achieve?

R **RELEVANT**	Why am I setting this goal now? Is it aligned with overall objectives?

T **TIME-BOUND**	What's the deadline and is it realistic?

SMART GOAL	Review what you have written, and craft a new goal statement based on what the answers to the questions above have revealed

INITIAL GOAL	Write the goal you have in mind
S **SPECIFIC**	What do you want to accomplish? Who needs to be included? When do you want to do this? Why is this a goal?
M **MEASURABLE**	How can you measure progress and know if you've successfully met your goal?
A **ACHIEVABLE**	Do you have the skills required to achieve the goal? If not, can you obtain them? What is the motivation for this goal? Is the amount of effort required on par with what the goal will achieve?
R **RELEVANT**	Why am I setting this goal now? Is it aligned with overall objectives?
T **TIME-BOUND**	What's the deadline and is it realistic?
SMART GOAL	Review what you have written, and craft a new goal statement based on what the answers to the questions above have revealed

INITIAL GOAL	Write the goal you have in mind

S / **SPECIFIC**	What do you want to accomplish? Who needs to be included? When do you want to do this? Why is this a goal?

M / **MEASURABLE**	How can you measure progress and know if you've successfully met your goal?

A / **ACHIEVABLE**	Do you have the skills required to achieve the goal? If not, can you obtain them? What is the motivation for this goal? Is the amount of effort required on par with what the goal will achieve?

R / **RELEVANT**	Why am I setting this goal now? Is it aligned with overall objectives?

T / **TIME-BOUND**	What's the deadline and is it realistic?

SMART GOAL	Review what you have written, and craft a new goal statement based on what the answers to the questions above have revealed

INITIAL GOAL	Write the goal you have in mind

S	What do you want to accomplish? Who needs to be included? When do you want to do this? Why is this a goal?
SPECIFIC	

M	How can you measure progress and know if you've successfully met your goal?
MEASURABLE	

A	Do you have the skills required to achieve the goal? If not, can you obtain them? What is the motivation for this goal? Is the amount of effort required on par with what the goal will achieve?
ACHIEVABLE	

R	Why am I setting this goal now? Is it aligned with overall objectives?
RELEVANT	

T	What's the deadline and is it realistic?
TIME-BOUND	

SMART GOAL	Review what you have written, and craft a new goal statement based on what the answers to the questions above have revealed

INITIAL GOAL	Write the goal you have in mind
S **SPECIFIC**	What do you want to accomplish? Who needs to be included? When do you want to do this? Why is this a goal?
M **MEASURABLE**	How can you measure progress and know if you've successfully met your goal?
A **ACHIEVABLE**	Do you have the skills required to achieve the goal? If not, can you obtain them? What is the motivation for this goal? Is the amount of effort required on par with what the goal will achieve?
R **RELEVANT**	Why am I setting this goal now? Is it aligned with overall objectives?
T **TIME-BOUND**	What's the deadline and is it realistic?
SMART GOAL	Review what you have written, and craft a new goal statement based on what the answers to the questions above have revealed

INITIAL GOAL	Write the goal you have in mind

S **SPECIFIC**	What do you want to accomplish? Who needs to be included? When do you want to do this? Why is this a goal?

M **MEASURABLE**	How can you measure progress and know if you've successfully met your goal?

A **ACHIEVABLE**	Do you have the skills required to achieve the goal? If not, can you obtain them? What is the motivation for this goal? Is the amount of effort required on par with what the goal will achieve?

R **RELEVANT**	Why am I setting this goal now? Is it aligned with overall objectives?

T **TIME-BOUND**	What's the deadline and is it realistic?

SMART GOAL	Review what you have written, and craft a new goal statement based on what the answers to the questions above have revealed

INITIAL GOAL

Write the goal you have in mind

S
SPECIFIC

What do you want to accomplish? Who needs to be included? When do you want to do this? Why is this a goal?

M
MEASURABLE

How can you measure progress and know if you've successfully met your goal?

A
ACHIEVABLE

Do you have the skills required to achieve the goal? If not, can you obtain them? What is the motivation for this goal? Is the amount of effort required on par with what the goal will achieve?

R
RELEVANT

Why am I setting this goal now? Is it aligned with overall objectives?

T
TIME-BOUND

What's the deadline and is it realistic?

SMART GOAL

Review what you have written, and craft a new goal statement based on what the answers to the questions above have revealed

INITIAL GOAL	Write the goal you have in mind

S **SPECIFIC**	What do you want to accomplish? Who needs to be included? When do you want to do this? Why is this a goal?

M **MEASURABLE**	How can you measure progress and know if you've successfully met your goal?

A **ACHIEVABLE**	Do you have the skills required to achieve the goal? If not, can you obtain them? What is the motivation for this goal? Is the amount of effort required on par with what the goal will achieve?

R **RELEVANT**	Why am I setting this goal now? Is it aligned with overall objectives?

T **TIME-BOUND**	What's the deadline and is it realistic?

SMART GOAL	Review what you have written, and craft a new goal statement based on what the answers to the questions above have revealed

INITIAL GOAL	Write the goal you have in mind

S SPECIFIC	What do you want to accomplish? Who needs to be included? When do you want to do this? Why is this a goal?

M MEASURABLE	How can you measure progress and know if you've successfully met your goal?

A ACHIEVABLE	Do you have the skills required to achieve the goal? If not, can you obtain them? What is the motivation for this goal? Is the amount of effort required on par with what the goal will achieve?

R RELEVANT	Why am I setting this goal now? Is it aligned with overall objectives?

T TIME-BOUND	What's the deadline and is it realistic?

SMART GOAL	Review what you have written, and craft a new goal statement based on what the answers to the questions above have revealed

INITIAL GOAL	Write the goal you have in mind

S	What do you want to accomplish? Who needs to be included? When do you want to do this? Why is this a goal?
SPECIFIC	

M	How can you measure progress and know if you've successfully met your goal?
MEASURABLE	

A	Do you have the skills required to achieve the goal? If not, can you obtain them? What is the motivation for this goal? Is the amount of effort required on par with what the goal will achieve?
ACHIEVABLE	

R	Why am I setting this goal now? Is it aligned with overall objectives?
RELEVANT	

T	What's the deadline and is it realistic?
TIME-BOUND	

SMART GOAL	Review what you have written, and craft a new goal statement based on what the answers to the questions above have revealed

INITIAL GOAL	Write the goal you have in mind

S SPECIFIC	What do you want to accomplish? Who needs to be included? When do you want to do this? Why is this a goal?

M MEASURABLE	How can you measure progress and know if you've successfully met your goal?

A ACHIEVABLE	Do you have the skills required to achieve the goal? If not, can you obtain them? What is the motivation for this goal? Is the amount of effort required on par with what the goal will achieve?

R RELEVANT	Why am I setting this goal now? Is it aligned with overall objectives?

T TIME-BOUND	What's the deadline and is it realistic?

SMART GOAL	Review what you have written, and craft a new goal statement based on what the answers to the questions above have revealed

INITIAL GOAL	Write the goal you have in mind
S **SPECIFIC**	What do you want to accomplish? Who needs to be included? When do you want to do this? Why is this a goal?
M **MEASURABLE**	How can you measure progress and know if you've successfully met your goal?
A **ACHIEVABLE**	Do you have the skills required to achieve the goal? If not, can you obtain them? What is the motivation for this goal? Is the amount of effort required on par with what the goal will achieve?
R **RELEVANT**	Why am I setting this goal now? Is it aligned with overall objectives?
T **TIME-BOUND**	What's the deadline and is it realistic?
SMART GOAL	Review what you have written, and craft a new goal statement based on what the answers to the questions above have revealed

INITIAL GOAL	Write the goal you have in mind

S	What do you want to accomplish? Who needs to be included? When do you want to do this? Why is this a goal?
SPECIFIC	

M	How can you measure progress and know if you've successfully met your goal?
MEASURABLE	

A	Do you have the skills required to achieve the goal? If not, can you obtain them? What is the motivation for this goal? Is the amount of effort required on par with what the goal will achieve?
ACHIEVABLE	

R	Why am I setting this goal now? Is it aligned with overall objectives?
RELEVANT	

T	What's the deadline and is it realistic?
TIME-BOUND	

SMART GOAL	Review what you have written, and craft a new goal statement based on what the answers to the questions above have revealed

INITIAL GOAL	Write the goal you have in mind

S SPECIFIC	What do you want to accomplish? Who needs to be included? When do you want to do this? Why is this a goal?

M MEASURABLE	How can you measure progress and know if you've successfully met your goal?

A ACHIEVABLE	Do you have the skills required to achieve the goal? If not, can you obtain them? What is the motivation for this goal? Is the amount of effort required on par with what the goal will achieve?

R RELEVANT	Why am I setting this goal now? Is it aligned with overall objectives?

T TIME-BOUND	What's the deadline and is it realistic?

SMART GOAL	Review what you have written, and craft a new goal statement based on what the answers to the questions above have revealed

INITIAL GOAL	Write the goal you have in mind

S	What do you want to accomplish? Who needs to be included? When do you want to do this? Why is this a goal?
SPECIFIC	

M	How can you measure progress and know if you've successfully met your goal?
MEASURABLE	

A	Do you have the skills required to achieve the goal? If not, can you obtain them? What is the motivation for this goal? Is the amount of effort required on par with what the goal will achieve?
ACHIEVABLE	

R	Why am I setting this goal now? Is it aligned with overall objectives?
RELEVANT	

T	What's the deadline and is it realistic?
TIME-BOUND	

SMART GOAL	Review what you have written, and craft a new goal statement based on what the answers to the questions above have revealed

INITIAL GOAL	Write the goal you have in mind
S	What do you want to accomplish? Who needs to be included? When do you want to do this? Why is this a goal?
SPECIFIC	
M	How can you measure progress and know if you've successfully met your goal?
MEASURABLE	
A	Do you have the skills required to achieve the goal? If not, can you obtain them? What is the motivation for this goal? Is the amount of effort required on par with what the goal will achieve?
ACHIEVABLE	
R	Why am I setting this goal now? Is it aligned with overall objectives?
RELEVANT	
T	What's the deadline and is it realistic?
TIME-BOUND	
SMART GOAL	Review what you have written, and craft a new goal statement based on what the answers to the questions above have revealed

INITIAL GOAL	Write the goal you have in mind

| S | What do you want to accomplish? Who needs to be included? When do you want to do this? Why is this a goal? |
| SPECIFIC | |

| M | How can you measure progress and know if you've successfully met your goal? |
| MEASURABLE | |

| A | Do you have the skills required to achieve the goal? If not, can you obtain them? What is the motivation for this goal? Is the amount of effort required on par with what the goal will achieve? |
| ACHIEVABLE | |

| R | Why am I setting this goal now? Is it aligned with overall objectives? |
| RELEVANT | |

| T | What's the deadline and is it realistic? |
| TIME-BOUND | |

| SMART GOAL | Review what you have written, and craft a new goal statement based on what the answers to the questions above have revealed |

INITIAL GOAL	Write the goal you have in mind
S	What do you want to accomplish? Who needs to be included? When do you want to do this? Why is this a goal?
SPECIFIC	
M	How can you measure progress and know if you've successfully met your goal?
MEASURABLE	
A	Do you have the skills required to achieve the goal? If not, can you obtain them? What is the motivation for this goal? Is the amount of effort required on par with what the goal will achieve?
ACHIEVABLE	
R	Why am I setting this goal now? Is it aligned with overall objectives?
RELEVANT	
T	What's the deadline and is it realistic?
TIME-BOUND	
SMART GOAL	Review what you have written, and craft a new goal statement based on what the answers to the questions above have revealed

INITIAL GOAL	Write the goal you have in mind

S	What do you want to accomplish? Who needs to be included? When do you want to do this? Why is this a goal?
SPECIFIC	

M	How can you measure progress and know if you've successfully met your goal?
MEASURABLE	

A	Do you have the skills required to achieve the goal? If not, can you obtain them? What is the motivation for this goal? Is the amount of effort required on par with what the goal will achieve?
ACHIEVABLE	

R	Why am I setting this goal now? Is it aligned with overall objectives?
RELEVANT	

T	What's the deadline and is it realistic?
TIME-BOUND	

SMART GOAL	Review what you have written, and craft a new goal statement based on what the answers to the questions above have revealed

INITIAL GOAL	Write the goal you have in mind

S	What do you want to accomplish? Who needs to be included? When do you want to do this? Why is this a goal?
SPECIFIC	

M	How can you measure progress and know if you've successfully met your goal?
MEASURABLE	

A	Do you have the skills required to achieve the goal? If not, can you obtain them? What is the motivation for this goal? Is the amount of effort required on par with what the goal will achieve?
ACHIEVABLE	

R	Why am I setting this goal now? Is it aligned with overall objectives?
RELEVANT	

T	What's the deadline and is it realistic?
TIME-BOUND	

SMART GOAL	Review what you have written, and craft a new goal statement based on what the answers to the questions above have revealed

INITIAL GOAL	Write the goal you have in mind

S	What do you want to accomplish? Who needs to be included? When do you want to do this? Why is this a goal?
SPECIFIC	

M	How can you measure progress and know if you've successfully met your goal?
MEASURABLE	

A	Do you have the skills required to achieve the goal? If not, can you obtain them? What is the motivation for this goal? Is the amount of effort required on par with what the goal will achieve?
ACHIEVABLE	

R	Why am I setting this goal now? Is it aligned with overall objectives?
RELEVANT	

T	What's the deadline and is it realistic?
TIME-BOUND	

SMART GOAL	Review what you have written, and craft a new goal statement based on what the answers to the questions above have revealed

INITIAL GOAL	Write the goal you have in mind
S **SPECIFIC**	What do you want to accomplish? Who needs to be included? When do you want to do this? Why is this a goal?
M **MEASURABLE**	How can you measure progress and know if you've successfully met your goal?
A **ACHIEVABLE**	Do you have the skills required to achieve the goal? If not, can you obtain them? What is the motivation for this goal? Is the amount of effort required on par with what the goal will achieve?
R **RELEVANT**	Why am I setting this goal now? Is it aligned with overall objectives?
T **TIME-BOUND**	What's the deadline and is it realistic?
SMART GOAL	Review what you have written, and craft a new goal statement based on what the answers to the questions above have revealed

INITIAL GOAL	Write the goal you have in mind

S SPECIFIC	What do you want to accomplish? Who needs to be included? When do you want to do this? Why is this a goal?

M MEASURABLE	How can you measure progress and know if you've successfully met your goal?

A ACHIEVABLE	Do you have the skills required to achieve the goal? If not, can you obtain them? What is the motivation for this goal? Is the amount of effort required on par with what the goal will achieve?

R RELEVANT	Why am I setting this goal now? Is it aligned with overall objectives?

T TIME-BOUND	What's the deadline and is it realistic?

SMART GOAL	Review what you have written, and craft a new goal statement based on what the answers to the questions above have revealed

	Write the goal you have in mind
INITIAL GOAL	

	What do you want to accomplish? Who needs to be included? When do you want to do this? Why is this a goal?
S	
SPECIFIC	

	How can you measure progress and know if you've successfully met your goal?
M	
MEASURABLE	

	Do you have the skills required to achieve the goal? If not, can you obtain them? What is the motivation for this goal? Is the amount of effort required on par with what the goal will achieve?
A	
ACHIEVABLE	

	Why am I setting this goal now? Is it aligned with overall objectives?
R	
RELEVANT	

	What's the deadline and is it realistic?
T	
TIME-BOUND	

	Review what you have written, and craft a new goal statement based on what the answers to the questions above have revealed
SMART GOAL	

INITIAL GOAL	Write the goal you have in mind

S SPECIFIC	What do you want to accomplish? Who needs to be included? When do you want to do this? Why is this a goal?

M MEASURABLE	How can you measure progress and know if you've successfully met your goal?

A ACHIEVABLE	Do you have the skills required to achieve the goal? If not, can you obtain them? What is the motivation for this goal? Is the amount of effort required on par with what the goal will achieve?

R RELEVANT	Why am I setting this goal now? Is it aligned with overall objectives?

T TIME-BOUND	What's the deadline and is it realistic?

SMART GOAL	Review what you have written, and craft a new goal statement based on what the answers to the questions above have revealed

INITIAL GOAL	Write the goal you have in mind
S	What do you want to accomplish? Who needs to be included? When do you want to do this? Why is this a goal?
SPECIFIC	
M	How can you measure progress and know if you've successfully met your goal?
MEASURABLE	
A	Do you have the skills required to achieve the goal? If not, can you obtain them? What is the motivation for this goal? Is the amount of effort required on par with what the goal will achieve?
ACHIEVABLE	
R	Why am I setting this goal now? Is it aligned with overall objectives?
RELEVANT	
T	What's the deadline and is it realistic?
TIME-BOUND	
SMART GOAL	Review what you have written, and craft a new goal statement based on what the answers to the questions above have revealed

INITIAL GOAL	Write the goal you have in mind

S	What do you want to accomplish? Who needs to be included? When do you want to do this? Why is this a goal?
SPECIFIC	

M	How can you measure progress and know if you've successfully met your goal?
MEASURABLE	

A	Do you have the skills required to achieve the goal? If not, can you obtain them? What is the motivation for this goal? Is the amount of effort required on par with what the goal will achieve?
ACHIEVABLE	

R	Why am I setting this goal now? Is it aligned with overall objectives?
RELEVANT	

T	What's the deadline and is it realistic?
TIME-BOUND	

SMART GOAL	Review what you have written, and craft a new goal statement based on what the answers to the questions above have revealed

INITIAL GOAL	Write the goal you have in mind

S **SPECIFIC**	What do you want to accomplish? Who needs to be included? When do you want to do this? Why is this a goal?

M **MEASURABLE**	How can you measure progress and know if you've successfully met your goal?

A **ACHIEVABLE**	Do you have the skills required to achieve the goal? If not, can you obtain them? What is the motivation for this goal? Is the amount of effort required on par with what the goal will achieve?

R **RELEVANT**	Why am I setting this goal now? Is it aligned with overall objectives?

T **TIME-BOUND**	What's the deadline and is it realistic?

SMART GOAL	Review what you have written, and craft a new goal statement based on what the answers to the questions above have revealed

INITIAL GOAL	Write the goal you have in mind
S **SPECIFIC**	What do you want to accomplish? Who needs to be included? When do you want to do this? Why is this a goal?
M **MEASURABLE**	How can you measure progress and know if you've successfully met your goal?
A **ACHIEVABLE**	Do you have the skills required to achieve the goal? If not, can you obtain them? What is the motivation for this goal? Is the amount of effort required on par with what the goal will achieve?
R **RELEVANT**	Why am I setting this goal now? Is it aligned with overall objectives?
T **TIME-BOUND**	What's the deadline and is it realistic?
SMART GOAL	Review what you have written, and craft a new goal statement based on what the answers to the questions above have revealed

INITIAL GOAL	Write the goal you have in mind
S **SPECIFIC**	What do you want to accomplish? Who needs to be included? When do you want to do this? Why is this a goal?
M **MEASURABLE**	How can you measure progress and know if you've successfully met your goal?
A **ACHIEVABLE**	Do you have the skills required to achieve the goal? If not, can you obtain them? What is the motivation for this goal? Is the amount of effort required on par with what the goal will achieve?
R **RELEVANT**	Why am I setting this goal now? Is it aligned with overall objectives?
T **TIME-BOUND**	What's the deadline and is it realistic?
SMART GOAL	Review what you have written, and craft a new goal statement based on what the answers to the questions above have revealed

INITIAL GOAL	Write the goal you have in mind
S **SPECIFIC**	What do you want to accomplish? Who needs to be included? When do you want to do this? Why is this a goal?
M **MEASURABLE**	How can you measure progress and know if you've successfully met your goal?
A **ACHIEVABLE**	Do you have the skills required to achieve the goal? If not, can you obtain them? What is the motivation for this goal? Is the amount of effort required on par with what the goal will achieve?
R **RELEVANT**	Why am I setting this goal now? Is it aligned with overall objectives?
T **TIME-BOUND**	What's the deadline and is it realistic?
SMART GOAL	Review what you have written, and craft a new goal statement based on what the answers to the questions above have revealed

INITIAL GOAL	Write the goal you have in mind
S **SPECIFIC**	What do you want to accomplish? Who needs to be included? When do you want to do this? Why is this a goal?
M **MEASURABLE**	How can you measure progress and know if you've successfully met your goal?
A **ACHIEVABLE**	Do you have the skills required to achieve the goal? If not, can you obtain them? What is the motivation for this goal? Is the amount of effort required on par with what the goal will achieve?
R **RELEVANT**	Why am I setting this goal now? Is it aligned with overall objectives?
T **TIME-BOUND**	What's the deadline and is it realistic?
SMART GOAL	Review what you have written, and craft a new goal statement based on what the answers to the questions above have revealed

INITIAL GOAL	Write the goal you have in mind

S	What do you want to accomplish? Who needs to be included? When do you want to do this? Why is this a goal?
SPECIFIC	

M	How can you measure progress and know if you've successfully met your goal?
MEASURABLE	

A	Do you have the skills required to achieve the goal? If not, can you obtain them? What is the motivation for this goal? Is the amount of effort required on par with what the goal will achieve?
ACHIEVABLE	

R	Why am I setting this goal now? Is it aligned with overall objectives?
RELEVANT	

T	What's the deadline and is it realistic?
TIME-BOUND	

SMART GOAL	Review what you have written, and craft a new goal statement based on what the answers to the questions above have revealed

INITIAL GOAL	Write the goal you have in mind
S **SPECIFIC**	What do you want to accomplish? Who needs to be included? When do you want to do this? Why is this a goal?
M **MEASURABLE**	How can you measure progress and know if you've successfully met your goal?
A **ACHIEVABLE**	Do you have the skills required to achieve the goal? If not, can you obtain them? What is the motivation for this goal? Is the amount of effort required on par with what the goal will achieve?
R **RELEVANT**	Why am I setting this goal now? Is it aligned with overall objectives?
T **TIME-BOUND**	What's the deadline and is it realistic?
SMART GOAL	Review what you have written, and craft a new goal statement based on what the answers to the questions above have revealed

INITIAL GOAL	Write the goal you have in mind

| S

SPECIFIC	What do you want to accomplish? Who needs to be included? When do you want to do this? Why is this a goal?

| M

MEASURABLE	How can you measure progress and know if you've successfully met your goal?

| A

ACHIEVABLE	Do you have the skills required to achieve the goal? If not, can you obtain them? What is the motivation for this goal? Is the amount of effort required on par with what the goal will achieve?

| R

RELEVANT	Why am I setting this goal now? Is it aligned with overall objectives?

| T

TIME-BOUND	What's the deadline and is it realistic?

SMART GOAL	Review what you have written, and craft a new goal statement based on what the answers to the questions above have revealed

INITIAL GOAL	Write the goal you have in mind

S **SPECIFIC**	What do you want to accomplish? Who needs to be included? When do you want to do this? Why is this a goal?

M **MEASURABLE**	How can you measure progress and know if you've successfully met your goal?

A **ACHIEVABLE**	Do you have the skills required to achieve the goal? If not, can you obtain them? What is the motivation for this goal? Is the amount of effort required on par with what the goal will achieve?

R **RELEVANT**	Why am I setting this goal now? Is it aligned with overall objectives?

T **TIME-BOUND**	What's the deadline and is it realistic?

SMART GOAL	Review what you have written, and craft a new goal statement based on what the answers to the questions above have revealed

INITIAL GOAL	Write the goal you have in mind

S SPECIFIC	What do you want to accomplish? Who needs to be included? When do you want to do this? Why is this a goal?

M MEASURABLE	How can you measure progress and know if you've successfully met your goal?

A ACHIEVABLE	Do you have the skills required to achieve the goal? If not, can you obtain them? What is the motivation for this goal? Is the amount of effort required on par with what the goal will achieve?

R RELEVANT	Why am I setting this goal now? Is it aligned with overall objectives?

T TIME-BOUND	What's the deadline and is it realistic?

SMART GOAL	Review what you have written, and craft a new goal statement based on what the answers to the questions above have revealed

INITIAL GOAL	Write the goal you have in mind
S **SPECIFIC**	What do you want to accomplish? Who needs to be included? When do you want to do this? Why is this a goal?
M **MEASURABLE**	How can you measure progress and know if you've successfully met your goal?
A **ACHIEVABLE**	Do you have the skills required to achieve the goal? If not, can you obtain them? What is the motivation for this goal? Is the amount of effort required on par with what the goal will achieve?
R **RELEVANT**	Why am I setting this goal now? Is it aligned with overall objectives?
T **TIME-BOUND**	What's the deadline and is it realistic?
SMART GOAL	Review what you have written, and craft a new goal statement based on what the answers to the questions above have revealed

INITIAL GOAL	Write the goal you have in mind

S	What do you want to accomplish? Who needs to be included? When do you want to do this? Why is this a goal?
SPECIFIC	

M	How can you measure progress and know if you've successfully met your goal?
MEASURABLE	

A	Do you have the skills required to achieve the goal? If not, can you obtain them? What is the motivation for this goal? Is the amount of effort required on par with what the goal will achieve?
ACHIEVABLE	

R	Why am I setting this goal now? Is it aligned with overall objectives?
RELEVANT	

T	What's the deadline and is it realistic?
TIME-BOUND	

SMART GOAL	Review what you have written, and craft a new goal statement based on what the answers to the questions above have revealed

INITIAL GOAL	Write the goal you have in mind

S	What do you want to accomplish? Who needs to be included? When do you want to do this? Why is this a goal?
SPECIFIC	

M	How can you measure progress and know if you've successfully met your goal?
MEASURABLE	

A	Do you have the skills required to achieve the goal? If not, can you obtain them? What is the motivation for this goal? Is the amount of effort required on par with what the goal will achieve?
ACHIEVABLE	

R	Why am I setting this goal now? Is it aligned with overall objectives?
RELEVANT	

T	What's the deadline and is it realistic?
TIME-BOUND	

SMART GOAL	Review what you have written, and craft a new goal statement based on what the answers to the questions above have revealed

INITIAL GOAL	Write the goal you have in mind
S **SPECIFIC**	What do you want to accomplish? Who needs to be included? When do you want to do this? Why is this a goal?
M **MEASURABLE**	How can you measure progress and know if you've successfully met your goal?
A **ACHIEVABLE**	Do you have the skills required to achieve the goal? If not, can you obtain them? What is the motivation for this goal? Is the amount of effort required on par with what the goal will achieve?
R **RELEVANT**	Why am I setting this goal now? Is it aligned with overall objectives?
T **TIME-BOUND**	What's the deadline and is it realistic?
SMART GOAL	Review what you have written, and craft a new goal statement based on what the answers to the questions above have revealed

INITIAL GOAL	Write the goal you have in mind
S **SPECIFIC**	What do you want to accomplish? Who needs to be included? When do you want to do this? Why is this a goal?
M **MEASURABLE**	How can you measure progress and know if you've successfully met your goal?
A **ACHIEVABLE**	Do you have the skills required to achieve the goal? If not, can you obtain them? What is the motivation for this goal? Is the amount of effort required on par with what the goal will achieve?
R **RELEVANT**	Why am I setting this goal now? Is it aligned with overall objectives?
T **TIME-BOUND**	What's the deadline and is it realistic?
SMART GOAL	Review what you have written, and craft a new goal statement based on what the answers to the questions above have revealed

INITIAL GOAL	Write the goal you have in mind
S **SPECIFIC**	What do you want to accomplish? Who needs to be included? When do you want to do this? Why is this a goal?
M **MEASURABLE**	How can you measure progress and know if you've successfully met your goal?
A **ACHIEVABLE**	Do you have the skills required to achieve the goal? If not, can you obtain them? What is the motivation for this goal? Is the amount of effort required on par with what the goal will achieve?
R **RELEVANT**	Why am I setting this goal now? Is it aligned with overall objectives?
T **TIME-BOUND**	What's the deadline and is it realistic?
SMART GOAL	Review what you have written, and craft a new goal statement based on what the answers to the questions above have revealed

| **INITIAL GOAL** | Write the goal you have in mind |
| | |

| **S** | What do you want to accomplish? Who needs to be included? When do you want to do this? Why is this a goal? |
| **SPECIFIC** | |

| **M** | How can you measure progress and know if you've successfully met your goal? |
| **MEASURABLE** | |

| **A** | Do you have the skills required to achieve the goal? If not, can you obtain them? What is the motivation for this goal? Is the amount of effort required on par with what the goal will achieve? |
| **ACHIEVABLE** | |

| **R** | Why am I setting this goal now? Is it aligned with overall objectives? |
| **RELEVANT** | |

| **T** | What's the deadline and is it realistic? |
| **TIME-BOUND** | |

| **SMART GOAL** | Review what you have written, and craft a new goal statement based on what the answers to the questions above have revealed |
| | |

INITIAL GOAL	Write the goal you have in mind

S	What do you want to accomplish? Who needs to be included? When do you want to do this? Why is this a goal?
SPECIFIC	

M	How can you measure progress and know if you've successfully met your goal?
MEASURABLE	

A	Do you have the skills required to achieve the goal? If not, can you obtain them? What is the motivation for this goal? Is the amount of effort required on par with what the goal will achieve?
ACHIEVABLE	

R	Why am I setting this goal now? Is it aligned with overall objectives?
RELEVANT	

T	What's the deadline and is it realistic?
TIME-BOUND	

SMART GOAL	Review what you have written, and craft a new goal statement based on what the answers to the questions above have revealed

INITIAL GOAL	Write the goal you have in mind

S	What do you want to accomplish? Who needs to be included? When do you want to do this? Why is this a goal?
SPECIFIC	

M	How can you measure progress and know if you've successfully met your goal?
MEASURABLE	

A	Do you have the skills required to achieve the goal? If not, can you obtain them? What is the motivation for this goal? Is the amount of effort required on par with what the goal will achieve?
ACHIEVABLE	

R	Why am I setting this goal now? Is it aligned with overall objectives?
RELEVANT	

T	What's the deadline and is it realistic?
TIME-BOUND	

SMART GOAL	Review what you have written, and craft a new goal statement based on what the answers to the questions above have revealed

INITIAL GOAL	Write the goal you have in mind

S	What do you want to accomplish? Who needs to be included? When do you want to do this? Why is this a goal?
SPECIFIC	

M	How can you measure progress and know if you've successfully met your goal?
MEASURABLE	

A	Do you have the skills required to achieve the goal? If not, can you obtain them? What is the motivation for this goal? Is the amount of effort required on par with what the goal will achieve?
ACHIEVABLE	

R	Why am I setting this goal now? Is it aligned with overall objectives?
RELEVANT	

T	What's the deadline and is it realistic?
TIME-BOUND	

SMART GOAL	Review what you have written, and craft a new goal statement based on what the answers to the questions above have revealed

INITIAL GOAL	Write the goal you have in mind

S	What do you want to accomplish? Who needs to be included? When do you want to do this? Why is this a goal?
SPECIFIC	

M	How can you measure progress and know if you've successfully met your goal?
MEASURABLE	

A	Do you have the skills required to achieve the goal? If not, can you obtain them? What is the motivation for this goal? Is the amount of effort required on par with what the goal will achieve?
ACHIEVABLE	

R	Why am I setting this goal now? Is it aligned with overall objectives?
RELEVANT	

T	What's the deadline and is it realistic?
TIME-BOUND	

SMART GOAL	Review what you have written, and craft a new goal statement based on what the answers to the questions above have revealed

INITIAL GOAL	Write the goal you have in mind

| S

SPECIFIC	What do you want to accomplish? Who needs to be included? When do you want to do this? Why is this a goal?

| M

MEASURABLE	How can you measure progress and know if you've successfully met your goal?

| A

ACHIEVABLE	Do you have the skills required to achieve the goal? If not, can you obtain them? What is the motivation for this goal? Is the amount of effort required on par with what the goal will achieve?

| R

RELEVANT	Why am I setting this goal now? Is it aligned with overall objectives?

| T

TIME-BOUND	What's the deadline and is it realistic?

SMART GOAL	Review what you have written, and craft a new goal statement based on what the answers to the questions above have revealed

INITIAL GOAL	Write the goal you have in mind

S	What do you want to accomplish? Who needs to be included? When do you want to do this? Why is this a goal?
SPECIFIC	

M	How can you measure progress and know if you've successfully met your goal?
MEASURABLE	

A	Do you have the skills required to achieve the goal? If not, can you obtain them? What is the motivation for this goal? Is the amount of effort required on par with what the goal will achieve?
ACHIEVABLE	

R	Why am I setting this goal now? Is it aligned with overall objectives?
RELEVANT	

T	What's the deadline and is it realistic?
TIME-BOUND	

SMART GOAL	Review what you have written, and craft a new goal statement based on what the answers to the questions above have revealed

INITIAL GOAL	Write the goal you have in mind

S **SPECIFIC**	What do you want to accomplish? Who needs to be included? When do you want to do this? Why is this a goal?

M **MEASURABLE**	How can you measure progress and know if you've successfully met your goal?

A **ACHIEVABLE**	Do you have the skills required to achieve the goal? If not, can you obtain them? What is the motivation for this goal? Is the amount of effort required on par with what the goal will achieve?

R **RELEVANT**	Why am I setting this goal now? Is it aligned with overall objectives?

T **TIME-BOUND**	What's the deadline and is it realistic?

SMART GOAL	Review what you have written, and craft a new goal statement based on what the answers to the questions above have revealed

INITIAL GOAL	Write the goal you have in mind
S **SPECIFIC**	What do you want to accomplish? Who needs to be included? When do you want to do this? Why is this a goal?
M **MEASURABLE**	How can you measure progress and know if you've successfully met your goal?
A **ACHIEVABLE**	Do you have the skills required to achieve the goal? If not, can you obtain them? What is the motivation for this goal? Is the amount of effort required on par with what the goal will achieve?
R **RELEVANT**	Why am I setting this goal now? Is it aligned with overall objectives?
T **TIME-BOUND**	What's the deadline and is it realistic?
SMART GOAL	Review what you have written, and craft a new goal statement based on what the answers to the questions above have revealed

INITIAL GOAL	Write the goal you have in mind

S	What do you want to accomplish? Who needs to be included? When do you want to do this? Why is this a goal?
SPECIFIC	

M	How can you measure progress and know if you've successfully met your goal?
MEASURABLE	

A	Do you have the skills required to achieve the goal? If not, can you obtain them? What is the motivation for this goal? Is the amount of effort required on par with what the goal will achieve?
ACHIEVABLE	

R	Why am I setting this goal now? Is it aligned with overall objectives?
RELEVANT	

T	What's the deadline and is it realistic?
TIME-BOUND	

SMART GOAL	Review what you have written, and craft a new goal statement based on what the answers to the questions above have revealed

INITIAL GOAL	Write the goal you have in mind

S	What do you want to accomplish? Who needs to be included? When do you want to do this? Why is this a goal?
SPECIFIC	

M	How can you measure progress and know if you've successfully met your goal?
MEASURABLE	

A	Do you have the skills required to achieve the goal? If not, can you obtain them? What is the motivation for this goal? Is the amount of effort required on par with what the goal will achieve?
ACHIEVABLE	

R	Why am I setting this goal now? Is it aligned with overall objectives?
RELEVANT	

T	What's the deadline and is it realistic?
TIME-BOUND	

SMART GOAL	Review what you have written, and craft a new goal statement based on what the answers to the questions above have revealed

INITIAL GOAL	Write the goal you have in mind

S	What do you want to accomplish? Who needs to be included? When do you want to do this? Why is this a goal?
SPECIFIC	

M	How can you measure progress and know if you've successfully met your goal?
MEASURABLE	

A	Do you have the skills required to achieve the goal? If not, can you obtain them? What is the motivation for this goal? Is the amount of effort required on par with what the goal will achieve?
ACHIEVABLE	

R	Why am I setting this goal now? Is it aligned with overall objectives?
RELEVANT	

T	What's the deadline and is it realistic?
TIME-BOUND	

SMART GOAL	Review what you have written, and craft a new goal statement based on what the answers to the questions above have revealed

INITIAL GOAL	Write the goal you have in mind

| S

SPECIFIC	What do you want to accomplish? Who needs to be included? When do you want to do this? Why is this a goal?

| M

MEASURABLE	How can you measure progress and know if you've successfully met your goal?

| A

ACHIEVABLE	Do you have the skills required to achieve the goal? If not, can you obtain them? What is the motivation for this goal? Is the amount of effort required on par with what the goal will achieve?

| R

RELEVANT	Why am I setting this goal now? Is it aligned with overall objectives?

| T

TIME-BOUND	What's the deadline and is it realistic?

SMART GOAL	Review what you have written, and craft a new goal statement based on what the answers to the questions above have revealed

INITIAL GOAL	Write the goal you have in mind

S **SPECIFIC**	What do you want to accomplish? Who needs to be included? When do you want to do this? Why is this a goal?

M **MEASURABLE**	How can you measure progress and know if you've successfully met your goal?

A **ACHIEVABLE**	Do you have the skills required to achieve the goal? If not, can you obtain them? What is the motivation for this goal? Is the amount of effort required on par with what the goal will achieve?

R **RELEVANT**	Why am I setting this goal now? Is it aligned with overall objectives?

T **TIME-BOUND**	What's the deadline and is it realistic?

SMART GOAL	Review what you have written, and craft a new goal statement based on what the answers to the questions above have revealed

INITIAL GOAL

Write the goal you have in mind

S
SPECIFIC

What do you want to accomplish? Who needs to be included? When do you want to do this? Why is this a goal?

M
MEASURABLE

How can you measure progress and know if you've successfully met your goal?

A
ACHIEVABLE

Do you have the skills required to achieve the goal? If not, can you obtain them? What is the motivation for this goal? Is the amount of effort required on par with what the goal will achieve?

R
RELEVANT

Why am I setting this goal now? Is it aligned with overall objectives?

T
TIME-BOUND

What's the deadline and is it realistic?

SMART GOAL

Review what you have written, and craft a new goal statement based on what the answers to the questions above have revealed

INITIAL GOAL	Write the goal you have in mind

S **SPECIFIC**	What do you want to accomplish? Who needs to be included? When do you want to do this? Why is this a goal?

M **MEASURABLE**	How can you measure progress and know if you've successfully met your goal?

A **ACHIEVABLE**	Do you have the skills required to achieve the goal? If not, can you obtain them? What is the motivation for this goal? Is the amount of effort required on par with what the goal will achieve?

R **RELEVANT**	Why am I setting this goal now? Is it aligned with overall objectives?

T **TIME-BOUND**	What's the deadline and is it realistic?

SMART GOAL	Review what you have written, and craft a new goal statement based on what the answers to the questions above have revealed

INITIAL GOAL	Write the goal you have in mind

S	What do you want to accomplish? Who needs to be included? When do you want to do this? Why is this a goal?
SPECIFIC	

M	How can you measure progress and know if you've successfully met your goal?
MEASURABLE	

A	Do you have the skills required to achieve the goal? If not, can you obtain them? What is the motivation for this goal? Is the amount of effort required on par with what the goal will achieve?
ACHIEVABLE	

R	Why am I setting this goal now? Is it aligned with overall objectives?
RELEVANT	

T	What's the deadline and is it realistic?
TIME-BOUND	

SMART GOAL	Review what you have written, and craft a new goal statement based on what the answers to the questions above have revealed

INITIAL GOAL	Write the goal you have in mind

| S

SPECIFIC	What do you want to accomplish? Who needs to be included? When do you want to do this? Why is this a goal?

| M

MEASURABLE	How can you measure progress and know if you've successfully met your goal?

| A

ACHIEVABLE	Do you have the skills required to achieve the goal? If not, can you obtain them? What is the motivation for this goal? Is the amount of effort required on par with what the goal will achieve?

| R

RELEVANT	Why am I setting this goal now? Is it aligned with overall objectives?

| T

TIME-BOUND	What's the deadline and is it realistic?

SMART GOAL	Review what you have written, and craft a new goal statement based on what the answers to the questions above have revealed

INITIAL GOAL	Write the goal you have in mind

S SPECIFIC	What do you want to accomplish? Who needs to be included? When do you want to do this? Why is this a goal?

M MEASURABLE	How can you measure progress and know if you've successfully met your goal?

A ACHIEVABLE	Do you have the skills required to achieve the goal? If not, can you obtain them? What is the motivation for this goal? Is the amount of effort required on par with what the goal will achieve?

R RELEVANT	Why am I setting this goal now? Is it aligned with overall objectives?

T TIME-BOUND	What's the deadline and is it realistic?

SMART GOAL	Review what you have written, and craft a new goal statement based on what the answers to the questions above have revealed

INITIAL GOAL	Write the goal you have in mind

S **SPECIFIC**	What do you want to accomplish? Who needs to be included? When do you want to do this? Why is this a goal?

M **MEASURABLE**	How can you measure progress and know if you've successfully met your goal?

A **ACHIEVABLE**	Do you have the skills required to achieve the goal? If not, can you obtain them? What is the motivation for this goal? Is the amount of effort required on par with what the goal will achieve?

R **RELEVANT**	Why am I setting this goal now? Is it aligned with overall objectives?

T **TIME-BOUND**	What's the deadline and is it realistic?

SMART GOAL	Review what you have written, and craft a new goal statement based on what the answers to the questions above have revealed

INITIAL GOAL

Write the goal you have in mind

S
SPECIFIC

What do you want to accomplish? Who needs to be included? When do you want to do this? Why is this a goal?

M
MEASURABLE

How can you measure progress and know if you've successfully met your goal?

A
ACHIEVABLE

Do you have the skills required to achieve the goal? If not, can you obtain them? What is the motivation for this goal? Is the amount of effort required on par with what the goal will achieve?

R
RELEVANT

Why am I setting this goal now? Is it aligned with overall objectives?

T
TIME-BOUND

What's the deadline and is it realistic?

SMART GOAL

Review what you have written, and craft a new goal statement based on what the answers to the questions above have revealed

INITIAL GOAL	Write the goal you have in mind

S	What do you want to accomplish? Who needs to be included? When do you want to do this? Why is this a goal?
SPECIFIC	

M	How can you measure progress and know if you've successfully met your goal?
MEASURABLE	

A	Do you have the skills required to achieve the goal? If not, can you obtain them? What is the motivation for this goal? Is the amount of effort required on par with what the goal will achieve?
ACHIEVABLE	

R	Why am I setting this goal now? Is it aligned with overall objectives?
RELEVANT	

T	What's the deadline and is it realistic?
TIME-BOUND	

SMART GOAL	Review what you have written, and craft a new goal statement based on what the answers to the questions above have revealed

INITIAL GOAL	Write the goal you have in mind

S	What do you want to accomplish? Who needs to be included? When do you want to do this? Why is this a goal?
SPECIFIC	

M	How can you measure progress and know if you've successfully met your goal?
MEASURABLE	

A	Do you have the skills required to achieve the goal? If not, can you obtain them? What is the motivation for this goal? Is the amount of effort required on par with what the goal will achieve?
ACHIEVABLE	

R	Why am I setting this goal now? Is it aligned with overall objectives?
RELEVANT	

T	What's the deadline and is it realistic?
TIME-BOUND	

SMART GOAL	Review what you have written, and craft a new goal statement based on what the answers to the questions above have revealed

INITIAL GOAL	Write the goal you have in mind

S	What do you want to accomplish? Who needs to be included? When do you want to do this? Why is this a goal?
SPECIFIC	

M	How can you measure progress and know if you've successfully met your goal?
MEASURABLE	

A	Do you have the skills required to achieve the goal? If not, can you obtain them? What is the motivation for this goal? Is the amount of effort required on par with what the goal will achieve?
ACHIEVABLE	

R	Why am I setting this goal now? Is it aligned with overall objectives?
RELEVANT	

T	What's the deadline and is it realistic?
TIME-BOUND	

SMART GOAL	Review what you have written, and craft a new goal statement based on what the answers to the questions above have revealed

INITIAL GOAL	Write the goal you have in mind

S	What do you want to accomplish? Who needs to be included? When do you want to do this? Why is this a goal?
SPECIFIC	

M	How can you measure progress and know if you've successfully met your goal?
MEASURABLE	

A	Do you have the skills required to achieve the goal? If not, can you obtain them? What is the motivation for this goal? Is the amount of effort required on par with what the goal will achieve?
ACHIEVABLE	

R	Why am I setting this goal now? Is it aligned with overall objectives?
RELEVANT	

T	What's the deadline and is it realistic?
TIME-BOUND	

SMART GOAL	Review what you have written, and craft a new goal statement based on what the answers to the questions above have revealed

INITIAL GOAL	Write the goal you have in mind

S **SPECIFIC**	What do you want to accomplish? Who needs to be included? When do you want to do this? Why is this a goal?

M **MEASURABLE**	How can you measure progress and know if you've successfully met your goal?

A **ACHIEVABLE**	Do you have the skills required to achieve the goal? If not, can you obtain them? What is the motivation for this goal? Is the amount of effort required on par with what the goal will achieve?

R **RELEVANT**	Why am I setting this goal now? Is it aligned with overall objectives?

T **TIME-BOUND**	What's the deadline and is it realistic?

SMART GOAL	Review what you have written, and craft a new goal statement based on what the answers to the questions above have revealed

INITIAL GOAL	Write the goal you have in mind

S	What do you want to accomplish? Who needs to be included? When do you want to do this? Why is this a goal?
SPECIFIC	

M	How can you measure progress and know if you've successfully met your goal?
MEASURABLE	

A	Do you have the skills required to achieve the goal? If not, can you obtain them? What is the motivation for this goal? Is the amount of effort required on par with what the goal will achieve?
ACHIEVABLE	

R	Why am I setting this goal now? Is it aligned with overall objectives?
RELEVANT	

T	What's the deadline and is it realistic?
TIME-BOUND	

SMART GOAL	Review what you have written, and craft a new goal statement based on what the answers to the questions above have revealed

INITIAL GOAL	Write the goal you have in mind

S SPECIFIC	What do you want to accomplish? Who needs to be included? When do you want to do this? Why is this a goal?

M MEASURABLE	How can you measure progress and know if you've successfully met your goal?

A ACHIEVABLE	Do you have the skills required to achieve the goal? If not, can you obtain them? What is the motivation for this goal? Is the amount of effort required on par with what the goal will achieve?

R RELEVANT	Why am I setting this goal now? Is it aligned with overall objectives?

T TIME-BOUND	What's the deadline and is it realistic?

SMART GOAL	Review what you have written, and craft a new goal statement based on what the answers to the questions above have revealed

INITIAL GOAL	Write the goal you have in mind
S **SPECIFIC**	What do you want to accomplish? Who needs to be included? When do you want to do this? Why is this a goal?
M **MEASURABLE**	How can you measure progress and know if you've successfully met your goal?
A **ACHIEVABLE**	Do you have the skills required to achieve the goal? If not, can you obtain them? What is the motivation for this goal? Is the amount of effort required on par with what the goal will achieve?
R **RELEVANT**	Why am I setting this goal now? Is it aligned with overall objectives?
T **TIME-BOUND**	What's the deadline and is it realistic?
SMART GOAL	Review what you have written, and craft a new goal statement based on what the answers to the questions above have revealed

INITIAL GOAL	Write the goal you have in mind

S SPECIFIC	What do you want to accomplish? Who needs to be included? When do you want to do this? Why is this a goal?

M MEASURABLE	How can you measure progress and know if you've successfully met your goal?

A ACHIEVABLE	Do you have the skills required to achieve the goal? If not, can you obtain them? What is the motivation for this goal? Is the amount of effort required on par with what the goal will achieve?

R RELEVANT	Why am I setting this goal now? Is it aligned with overall objectives?

T TIME-BOUND	What's the deadline and is it realistic?

SMART GOAL	Review what you have written, and craft a new goal statement based on what the answers to the questions above have revealed

INITIAL GOAL	Write the goal you have in mind

S **SPECIFIC**	What do you want to accomplish? Who needs to be included? When do you want to do this? Why is this a goal?

M **MEASURABLE**	How can you measure progress and know if you've successfully met your goal?

A **ACHIEVABLE**	Do you have the skills required to achieve the goal? If not, can you obtain them? What is the motivation for this goal? Is the amount of effort required on par with what the goal will achieve?

R **RELEVANT**	Why am I setting this goal now? Is it aligned with overall objectives?

T **TIME-BOUND**	What's the deadline and is it realistic?

SMART GOAL	Review what you have written, and craft a new goal statement based on what the answers to the questions above have revealed

Made in the USA
Coppell, TX
07 November 2024

39818066R10057